MORE FREAKY ANIMAL STORIES

BY JANEY LEVY

Gareth Stevens
PUBLISHING

Please visit our website, www.garethstevens.com. For a free color catalog of all our high-quality books, call toll free 1-800-542-2595 or fax 1-877-542-2596.

Library of Congress Cataloging-in-Publication Data

Names: Levy, Janey, author.
Title: More freaky animal stories / Janey Levy.
Description: New York : Gareth Stevens Publishing, [2020] | Series: Freaky true science | Includes index.
Identifiers: LCCN 2018057435| ISBN 9781538240540 (paperback) | ISBN 9781538240564 (library bound) | ISBN 9781538240557 (6 pack)
Subjects: LCSH: Animals–Miscellanea–Juvenile literature.
Classification: LCC QL49 .L3866 2020 | DDC 590–dc23
LC record available at https://lccn.loc.gov/2018057435

First Edition

Published in 2020 by
Gareth Stevens Publishing
111 East 14th Street, Suite 349
New York, NY 10003

Designer: Sarah Liddell
Editor: Therese Shea

Photo credits: Cover, p. 1 (frog) Davidvraju/Wikimedia Commons; cover, p. 1 (tail) AKaiser/Shutterstock.com; cover, background used throughout andreiuc88/ Shutterstock.com; wing used throughout Mur34/Shutterstock.com; hand used throughout Helena Ohman/Shutterstock.com; paper texture used throughout Alex Gontar/ Shutterstock.com; p. 5 Gerald A. DeBoer/Shutterstock.com; p. 7 Yiming Chen/Moment/ Getty Images; p. 9 gilkop/Shutterstock.com; p. 11 Dave Fleetham/Perspectives/ Getty Images; p. 13 Tortie tude/Wikimedia Commons; p. 15 WolfmanSF/Wikimedia Commons; p. 17 Reluk/Shutterstock.com; p. 19 Sandesh Kadur/Nature Picture Library/ Nature Picture Library/Getty Images; p. 21 Janusz Baczynski/Shutterstock.com; p. 23 John Carnemolla/Shutterstock.com; p. 25 Chris Jackson/Staff/Getty Images Entertainment/ Getty Images; p. 27 Anadolu Agency/Contributor/Anadolu Agency/Getty Images; p. 29 (glass octopus) Citron/Wikimedia Commons; p. 29 (dumbo octopus) Heinonlein/ Wikimedia Commons; p. 29 (tardigrade) 3Dstock/Shutterstock.com; p. 29 (translucent snail) Innotata/Wikimedia Commons; p. 29 (glass butterfly) David Tiller/ Wikimedia Commons; p. 29 (tarsier) Bambara/Shutterstock.com; p. 29 (crow) Mdf/ Wikimedia Commons.

Printed in the United States of America.

CPSIA compliance information: Batch #CS19GS: For further information contact Gareth Stevens, New York, New York at 1-800-542-2595.

CONTENTS

Words in the glossary appear in **bold** type
the first time they are used in the text.

THE WORLD OF ANIMALS

Did you ever wonder why certain organisms are called animals? What does that mean? And how are animals different than plants? Unlike plants, animals can't make their own food. They must eat other organisms. Animals breathe oxygen and give off a gas called carbon dioxide. Most animals can move around freely. Animals are usually made of many cells, and these cells are different than plant cells.

Not even scientists know exactly how many animal species exist. About 1.3 million species have been identified, and researchers believe there may be more than 8 million in all. Many animals are pretty freaky, such as the immortal jellyfish, and there are some freaky animal stories, too. Did you know bees followed a car for 2 days to perform a rescue? Inside this book, you'll discover more about the freaky side of animals!

FREAKY FACTS!

The first animal on Earth may have been a sea sponge that appeared about 640 million years ago.

MANY CELLS IN YOUR BODY AREN'T ACTUALLY YOU

You probably don't think of yourself as an animal, but you are! Here's a freaky fact about you and every other human animal. On and inside you live **trillions**—*trillions*—of organisms. These microscopic organisms are bacteria. But don't be alarmed. These bacteria are helpful, not harmful. They perform tasks such as protecting you from disease and helping with **digestion**. The large intestine alone may have over 500 species of bacteria. It's estimated you have more bacteria cells than human cells!

ANOTHER FEATURE OF MOST ANIMALS
IS THAT THEY MATE AND REPRODUCE.

5

THE INCREDIBLE IMMORTAL JELLYFISH

In the normal course of events, living creatures are born, live their lives, and then die, right? That may be true for most creatures, but not for the jellyfish *Turritopsis dohrnii*, popularly known as the immortal jellyfish.

Like all jellyfish, the immortal jellyfish begins life as a larva. It then attaches itself to the seafloor and becomes a **polyp**. Finally, it grows into the familiar adult form—a bell with **tentacles** hanging from it. And the adults start making babies.

Death should come next, but not for immortal jellyfish. How do they avoid dying? They change back into their immature form! First they change into a tiny blob, then within 3 days, they change back into their polyp form. They can do this over and over again.

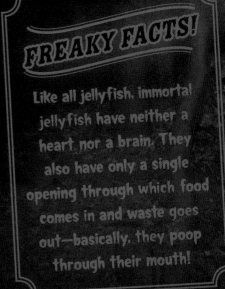

FREAKY FACTS!

Like all jellyfish, immortal jellyfish have neither a heart nor a brain. They also have only a single opening through which food comes in and waste goes out—basically, they poop through their mouth!

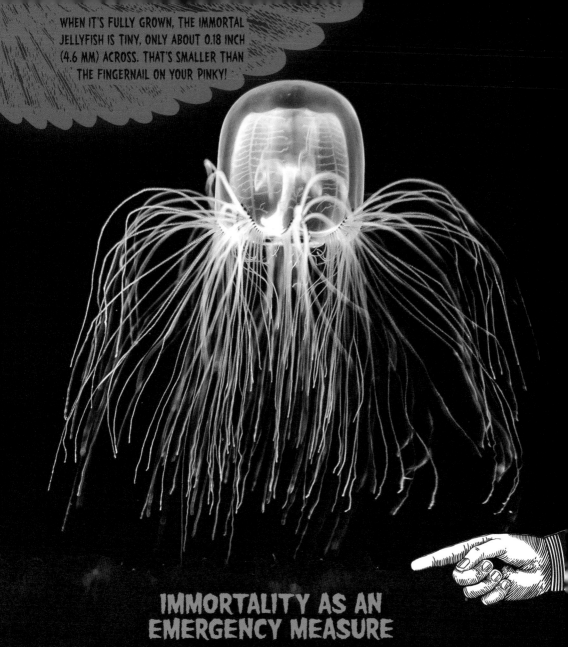

WHEN IT'S FULLY GROWN, THE IMMORTAL JELLYFISH IS TINY, ONLY ABOUT 0.18 INCH (4.6 MM) ACROSS. THAT'S SMALLER THAN THE FINGERNAIL ON YOUR PINKY!

IMMORTALITY AS AN EMERGENCY MEASURE

The immortality measures of *Turritopsis dohrnii* are triggered only under certain conditions. If the jellyfish is starving, has suffered physical damage, or finds itself in surroundings that are harmful to it, it changes back into its immature form. Scientists call the process of rebuilding tissues regeneration. But regeneration isn't the same as true immortality, which means never dying. Immortal jellyfish can be eaten by other organisms or die of diseases.

MOKO
THE DOLPHIN
TO THE RESCUE

Bottlenose dolphins are social animals that live in groups. So when a lone dolphin made his home along a New Zealand beach, scientists believed he'd become separated from his group. The dolphin became famous for playing with swimmers, and locals named him Moko. Then, in 2008, Moko became famous for an amazing rescue.

Two pygmy sperm whales became stranded on the beach where Moko had long played. A nearby sandbar confused them, and they couldn't find their way out to sea. Human rescuers tried to help them, but failed and feared the whales would die. Suddenly Moko, who had heard the whales' distress calls, appeared. Although Moko and the whales were different species, Moko was able to communicate with them, and they followed him safely out to sea!

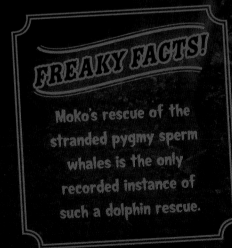

FREAKY FACTS!

Moko's rescue of the stranded pygmy sperm whales is the only recorded instance of such a dolphin rescue.

BEACHED WHALES

When whales strand themselves on a beach, they're said to beach
themselves. About 700 whales beach themselves in New Zealand
every year. Lots of theories exist for why whales do this, although
no one knows for sure. Some researchers believe navy sonar
confuses them. Other possible causes that have been suggested
include illnesses, parasites, genetic mutations, injuries, and old age.
Beached whales often can't be saved and must be killed to prevent
them from suffering a terrible death.

THE UNICORN OF THE SEA

The unicorn is a wondrous animal of legend, with a horselike body and a single long, straight horn in the middle of its forehead. It doesn't exist. But the unicorn of the sea is a real, live marine mammal called a narwhal.

Narwhals are toothed whales related to bottlenose dolphins, harbor porpoises, killer whales, and beluga whales. What sets them apart from their relatives and makes them so extraordinary is a highly unusual tooth. Males have a tooth that grows right through their upper lip (ouch!) into a swordlike, **spiral** tusk. The tusk grows to be 9 to 10 feet (2.7 to 3 m) long! The tusk's purpose has been something of a mystery. It may be used to hunt fish or detect the level of salt in the water.

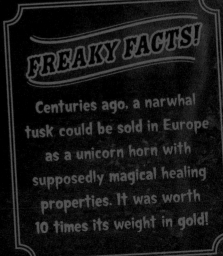

FREAKY FACTS!

Centuries ago, a narwhal tusk could be sold in Europe as a unicorn horn with supposedly magical healing properties. It was worth 10 times its weight in gold!

MOST OF THE TIME, MALE NARWHALS
HAVE ONE TUSK AND FEMALES HAVE NONE.
RARELY, A MALE WILL GROW TWO TUSKS.
EQUALLY RARELY, A FEMALE
WILL GROW A TUSK.

THE NARWHAL'S REMARKABLE TUSK

Ten million **nerve** connections run between the central nerve in the narwhal's tusk and its outer surface. These enable the tusk to detect changes in water temperature and pressure. The tusk can also detect changes in the numbers of particles in the water, and this allows narwhals to identify particles that come from the fish they eat. Nothing else like the narwhal tusk is known.

INKY, THE OCTOPUS HOUDINI

Inky, a male common New Zealand octopus, lived at the National Aquarium of New Zealand, where he'd been since 2014. Inky was popular with aquarium staff and visitors because he was so friendly, curious, and intelligent. But then one morning in 2016, Inky wasn't there.

Inky wasn't stolen. Rather, he used his intelligence to make a breakout worthy of any great escape artist. Wet tracks on the floor told the tale. During the night, Inky escaped his tank through just a small gap left at the top. He dropped to the floor, then slid about 8 feet (2.4 m) across it to a drainpipe. He then plopped into the pipe and slid 164 feet (50 m) down it into the ocean and freedom!

EVEN THOUGH INKY'S BODY IS ABOUT THE SIZE OF A FOOTBALL, HE WAS ABLE TO SQUEEZE THROUGH THE SMALL SPACE AT THE TOP OF HIS TANK BECAUSE OCTOPUSES HAVE SOFT, BONELESS BODIES.

MORE INCREDIBLE OCTOPUS TALES

Many stories provide evidence of octopuses' intelligence. At a marine education center in Wellington, New Zealand, an octopus regularly left its tank at night to steal crabs from another tank, then returned to its own tank. In California, an octopus caused a flood when it pointed a tube to shoot water out of its tank for 10 hours. Another octopus took a robot submarine apart piece by piece. And these are just a few of the remarkable octopus tales!

DEEP-SEA GIANT TUBE WORMS

In 1977, scientists exploring a deep-sea **hydrothermal vent** in the Pacific Ocean were astonished to discover life flourishing there. They had believed conditions around these vents made life impossible. Yet life was abundant—including, most notably, giant tube worms.

Giant tube worms are extremely strange animals. They live at depths up to 1.6 miles (2.6 km), in total darkness, and in waters low in oxygen, high in toxic chemicals, and heated above 750°F (400°C)!

Each worm lives inside a long, narrow tube attached to the ocean floor. The tube is made of chitin (KY-tuhn), which is also found in the hard outer covering of insects, crabs, and lobsters. But the worm's most notable feature is its bright red, feather-like organ, which floats above the tube, but withdraws inside it when threatened.

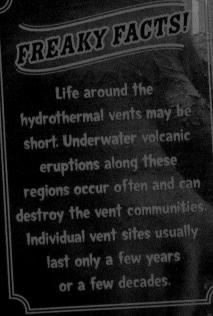

FREAKY FACTS!

Life around the hydrothermal vents may be short. Underwater volcanic eruptions along these regions occur often and can destroy the vent communities. Individual vent sites usually last only a few years or a few decades.

IN THE HARSH CONDITIONS AROUND THE
HYDROTHERMAL VENTS, GIANT TUBE WORMS GROW
RAPIDLY. THEY'RE ONE OF THE FASTEST-GROWING
ORGANISMS ON EARTH AND CAN GROW WELL
OVER 3 FEET (0.9 M) IN JUST 1 YEAR.

WHAT'S FOR DINNER?

With no mouth or gut, giant tube worms can't eat. So how do
they get the nutrients they need to live and grow? They have
a symbiotic relationship with bacteria living inside them. That
is, they have a relationship with the bacteria in which they both
benefit. Through the worms' bright red, feather-like organ,
they take in chemicals from the water that feed the bacteria. In
return, the bacteria turn the chemicals into food for the worms.
Everyone wins!

BIZARRE BEE SWARM

Carol Howarth, who lives in the United Kingdom, was having a nice day. She visited a nature reserve, then stopped in town to shop. But things took a strange turn when she returned to her car. It was covered with bees!

A swarm of about 20,000 bees coated the back end of Carol's car. A park ranger driving by stopped to help. He called beekeepers, who came and removed the bees. All seemed well, and Carol drove home. But the next morning, the bees were back! Carol had to call the beekeepers again.

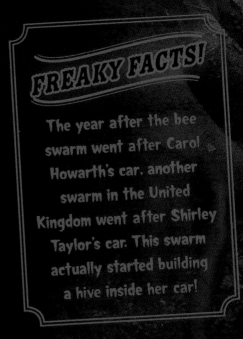

FREAKY FACTS!

The year after the bee swarm went after Carol Howarth's car, another swarm in the United Kingdom went after Shirley Taylor's car. This swarm actually started building a hive inside her car!

What caused the bee swarm? The beekeepers believe the queen bee got trapped in Carol's car, or left her scent there, causing the bees to follow the car to try to rescue her.

WHY SAVE THE QUEEN?

The queen bee is the center of the hive. She's the only queen in a colony that may have 60,000 or more bees. She's the mother of those bees. Her job is to lay eggs to make more bees, and most of the other bees work to support her egg laying. Without her, there is no colony, so the other bees will go to any lengths to protect her.

IMAGINE HAVING A SWARM OF BEES
LIKE THIS COVERING YOUR CAR!

17

THE PECULIAR PURPLE FROG

Everyone knows what frogs are like. They're amphibians that hop around on the ground. They're greenish or brightly colored, like poison dart frogs, and have a large head and wide mouth. But that concept doesn't fit a frog scientists found in India in 2003. The purple, or pig-nosed, frog is a very peculiar creature.

The purple frog is, not surprisingly, dark purple or sometimes brownish. Its body is large and swollen looking. The head is small and seems too short for the body. It has small eyes, a narrow mouth, and a narrow snout that ends in a little white bulb. Its short legs aren't good for jumping. It's a burrowing animal that spends its life underground, coming to the surface just once a year for a few weeks to seek a mate.

FREAKY FACTS!

Although scientists only found the purple frog in 2003, it's been known to the people of India for centuries as a medical remedy. It's eaten as a treatment for the breathing problem known as asthma.

UNDERGROUND HUNTING

Adult purple frogs dine on termites underground. How do they find
their prey? They don't hunt by sight. Their small eyes aren't well
developed, and they don't have good vision. However, their odd snout
is touch sensitive, so they depend on touch and smell as they hunt.
Once they locate termite tunnels, they break into those tunnels and
use their grooved tongue to suck up the termites. Yum!

WOJTEK,
THE WARRIOR BEAR

It was 1942 in Europe, the middle of World War II. Polish soldiers passing through Iran encountered a young boy caring for an orphaned bear cub. Seeing that the cub was hungry, the soldiers bought him from the boy and took him with them. They named him Wojtek, which means "happy warrior." He learned to salute and even take showers by himself!

Wojtek became most famous for events during a big battle in 1944. Terrified by the noise of the fighting, Wojtek first climbed a tree. But when he saw his friends carrying crates of **ammunition**, he came down to help. He stood up on his hind legs and held out his two front legs. Then, he actually carried ammunition crates during the battle!

FREAKY FACTS!

During the war, Wojtek often got into trouble. He stole clothes hanging out to dry, ate the food meant for the soldiers' Christmas feast, and got stuck up a palm tree.

WOJTEK AFTER THE WAR

After the war ended, many of the Polish soldiers chose to go to Scotland rather than return to Poland. They took Wojtek with them. He stayed with the soldiers at a settlement camp for a while, then moved to the Edinburgh Zoo. Whenever he heard a zoo visitor speaking Polish, he would stand on his hind legs and wave. Wojteck lived at the zoo until his death in 1963, when he was 21 or 22 years old.

THE PERPLEXING PLATYPUS

Platypuses were well known to Australia's Aboriginal, or native, people. But when British scientists first saw a specimen, they thought it was a hoax. Who can blame them? The creatures have an otter's body and fur, a duck's bill and webbed feet, and a beaver's tail. But this animal is no hoax.

The platypus is one of only two mammals that lay eggs and one of the few mammals with venom, or poison. Males have a spur on each ankle that delivers the venom in fights. The platypus's body is perfectly designed for its life hunting food underwater. Their fur keeps them warm, and they paddle with their webbed feet. They find food with their bill, which detects movement and the electric fields produced by living things.

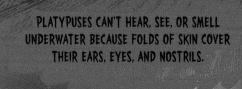

DINING SECRETS

Platypuses eat shellfish, insects, larvae, and worms they find
in the muddy bottom of the body of water they're swimming in.
They scoop them up in their bill, then swim to the surface to eat.
BUT—platypuses have no teeth. So to smash up their food into
small pieces, they use gravel they've scooped up with their food.
Once they've smashed up their food, they swallow it, and it goes
straight from their throat to their intestines—because platypuses
have no stomach!

DAISY, THE CANCER-DETECTING DOG

Dogs have an astonishing sense of smell. It's at least 10,000 times better than humans' sense of smell! In 2008, Claire Guest founded Medical Detection Dogs to put dogs' sense of smell to work helping human patients. She believed dogs could be trained to detect **cancer**, but few doctors believed her. Little did Claire know her own dog Daisy's sense of smell would provide the proof she needed.

One day in 2009, Daisy kept pawing and bumping Claire's chest. She pushed so hard she bruised Claire. Daisy's behavior was so odd Claire decided to see her doctor. Tests showed a very deep cancer, one that wouldn't have produced a noticeable lump for years. By then, it would have been much more deadly. Daisy had saved Claire's life.

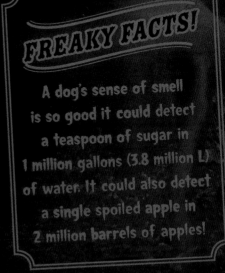

FREAKY FACTS!

A dog's sense of smell is so good it could detect a teaspoon of sugar in 1 million gallons (3.8 million L) of water. It could also detect a single spoiled apple in 2 million barrels of apples!

MEDICAL DETECTION DOGS WAS HONORED BY THE BRITISH ROYAL FAMILY, AND DAISY MET CAMILLA, THE DUCHESS OF CORNWALL.

A LIFE OF SUCCESS

After detecting Claire's cancer, Daisy went on to do the work Claire had dreamed of. Dogs at Medical Detection Dogs are trained to sniff breath and pee samples to detect cancer. Daisy sniffed over 6,500 samples and detected 550 cases of cancer. Her success rate was about 94 percent. Daisy retired from her detection duties in 2016 and died in 2018, but Medical Detection Dogs continues its work.

THE UNIQUE EURASIAN WRYNECK

Imagine you're a bird that finds itself in danger. How do you protect yourself? Do you fly away? Do you attack the threat with your bill? Either of these would make sense. But a small woodpecker called the Eurasian wryneck does something you wouldn't expect. It pretends to be a snake!

When threatened, Eurasian wrynecks bend and twist their heads and necks from side to side in a snakelike manner. They even hiss like a snake would. Now, you might think a feathered bird pretending to be a scaly snake wouldn't be a very effective defense. But deep in the forest, with the wryneck hiding inside a dark hole in a tree, its twisting and hissing is convincing enough to scare off predators!

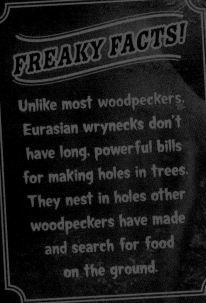

FREAKY FACTS!

Unlike most woodpeckers, Eurasian wrynecks don't have long, powerful bills for making holes in trees. They nest in holes other woodpeckers have made and search for food on the ground.

THE EURASIAN WRYNECK'S SCIENTIFIC NAME IS *JYNX TORQUILLA*. *TORQUILLA* COMES FROM A LATIN WORD MEANING "TO TWIST."

BEWITCHING BIRDS

Because of their unusual behavior when threatened, Eurasian wrynecks were once thought to have magical powers and were associated with witchcraft and spells. Some even thought the birds' powers were evil. They were once known as jynx birds, and *Jynx* is still part of their scientific name. From that, we get our modern word *jinx*, which means "one that brings bad luck."

FREAKY, AMAZING ANIMALS

The animal world is a wonderful place, full of amazing and sometimes freaky creatures. This book has covered some of them, but many, many more exist. Here are just a few additional examples.

Tardigrades are nearly microscopic animals that can survive anywhere, even in space! Some sea creatures, such as the glass octopus and the glass squid, hide from predators by being transparent, making it hard to see them. Small mammals called tarsiers have huge eyes that see so well in the dark they've been called night-vision goggles.

Now that you've learned about some freaky animals and discovered more exist, are you curious to learn more? Keep digging, and do your own research! Who knows what you'll discover about the amazing animal world?

FREAKY FACTS!

Each of the tarsier's eyes is as big as its brain!

MORE FREAKY ANIMALS

GLASS
OCTOPUS

DUMBO
OCTOPUS

TARDIGRADE

GLASSWING
BUTTERFLY

TARSIER

TRANSLUCENT
SNAIL

MORE ANIMAL FREAKINESS

A very strange thing happened one day at the zoo in Budapest, Hungary. A crow was drowning in the pool inside the area where the brown bears lived. The female bear noticed the crow, grabbed it by its wing with her teeth, and lifted it out of the water. But the bear didn't hurt the crow or try to eat it. She returned to eating her carrots and apples. The crow recovered and flew away!

GLOSSARY

ammunition: bullets, shells, and other things fired by weapons

cancer: a disease caused by the uncontrolled growth of cells in the body

digestion: the process of breaking down food inside the body so that the body can use it

hydrothermal vent: a break in the ocean floor where seawater is heated by magma to extremely high temperatures

nerve: a part of the body that sends messages between the brain and other parts of the body

nutrient: something a living thing needs to grow and stay alive

polyp: a small sea animal that has a body shaped like a tube

sonar: a machine that uses sound waves to find things in a body of water

spiral: a shape or line that curls outward from a center point

tentacle: a long, thin body part that sticks out from an animal's head or mouth

trillion: one thousand billion, or 1,000,000,000,000

FOR MORE INFORMATION

BOOKS

McGhee, Karen. *Australia's Most Freaky*. Sydney, Australia: Australian Geographic, 2014.

O'Brien, Lindsy. *The World's Weirdest Animals*. Mankato, MN: Capstone Press, 2015.

Tarakson, Stella. *Freaky Animals*. Broomall, PA: Mason Crest, 2018.

WEBSITES

10 Weird and Wonderful Wildlife of Australia
www.natureaustralia.org.au/celebrating-australia/
10-weird-and-wonderful-wildlife-of-australia/
Learn about some of Australia's most unusual animals on this site, and see pictures of them.

10 Weirdest, Most Bizarre Animals Found
www.conservationinstitute.org/10-weirdest-bizarre-animals-found/
Discover more freaky animals here, along with their photographs.

10 Weird Little Aliens You Can Find Right Here on Earth
www.popsci.com/weirdest-alien-animals
This website introduces you to even more freaky creatures.

INDEX